Y0-DBO-349

SENIOR
MOMENTS

Growing Old Is NOT For Sissies

Don Core

Illustrations by Chet Dickenson

© by Don Core 1999

Pubished by:

SOFITS Publishing
Post Office Box 65235
Vancouver, WA 98665

Drawings and Illustrations by
Chet Dickenson

Printed in the United States of America

Core, Don
   SENIOR MOMENTS; Growing Old is NOT for Sissies
   / by Don Core
   1. Aging—Humor.   I Title
   814.54   LC 99-90399

ISBN 1-879752-03-4
   First edition

What others are saying about this book:

Senior Moments is an absolute delight. You want Patrick McManus meets The Sunshine Boys? You got it! Core's irreverent and hilarious look at aging will move and amuse you at the same time. You'll relate, whatever your age; if you're not a senior, with luck you will be. This one, I say, is a must-read.
Carolyn K. Brock
Cala Creek Consumer Alert Book Reviewer

"Senior Moments" is the story of a century in transition and of ordinary people who accomplished extraordinary things. It is written with insight, wisdom and humor and offers a heartwarming chronicle of the way we were.
J.L. Dinsmore

I enjoyed this book so much because I can really relate to it. At times I laughed so hard it brought tears to my eyes.
Illa J. Dickenson

I got a lot of chuckles from the book - and felt a lot of 'that happened to me.' I know I am getting older when I can read about senior moments and relate to everything!!! HA HA....
PatBud (my new name) *Clark*

In Memory of

Ralph L. Core

my younger brother, by four
years, who worked for forty
plus years, paying into Social
Security, and never lived long
enough to receive any of the
benefits.   Think about it.

Acknowledgments

This book contains a number of "one-liners," some of which have been around since Day One. A few were written by two of my favorite authors, Anonymous and Unknown. I felt they were worth repeating as they seem appropriate. Thanks for your help folks.

Also, a very special acknowledgment to Kathryn G., my very own live-in editor, spell-checker, grammarian, cheering section, love of my life, wife and buddy (without whom I am just another creative loose cannon), hereinafter referred to as WifeBud.

I would also like to thank the Pulitzer nominating committee for . . . . . No? Oh.

I would also like to thank the Academy nominating committee. I will cherish Oscar . . . . . No? Oh.

Well, what then? I did a lot of work around here, don't you know? That ought to be worth som . . . . . Oh.

All right, I will sit down. But I won't be quiet.
Take a look at this . . . . .

Contents

ONE

The morning ritual

For so many senior citizens, the days start out pretty much the same. "I would have loved to sleep in a bit this morning," I said to nobody in particular. There is just WifeBud and I in the whole place.

"Did you get a good night's sleep, Dear?" inquired WifeBud.

"It could have been a lot better," I replied, "I must have been up a dozen times draining my tank." The actual number of trips to the bathroom during the night was a lot closer to three, maybe four if I had downed that extra brew the previous evening.

"Yeah," I thought to myself, "I've got to keep tabs on the old prostate, I don't want those knife-happy saw-bones types messing with my private parts."

"How did you sleep, WifeBud?" I inquired. I mean

to be democratic about this morning ritual and give her a chance to join in the morning inventory of parts and functions.

"Like a log," WifeBud replied, "now if I can just get my stomach to start acting the way it should."

"Not another day of feeling yucky, I hope. You would think with all the medical technology of today, doctors could find a treatment for yucky," I offered.

"You would think so; this is getting to be so tiring. Doctors don't seem to understand 'yucky.' My lady friends know exactly what I am talking about when I say 'yucky.' Anyhow, how are you feeling this morning, Dear? Is your back still bothering you? And how about your arthritis?"

Parts and functions discussions like this take about an hour each morning. It's always advisable to determine if everything is in proper working order early on in the day. It would put a serious damper on your whole day if you didn't find out until three o'clock in the afternoon that your blood had quit pumping through your veins some time during the night. Once a full inventory of parts and functions has been completed, we are ready to go on to more mundane discussions.

"What's on today's docket, WifeBud?" I ask, trying

to determine what is in store for me before I make any kind of commitment. I can be just as cagey as anyone. "I'm playing bridge with the ladies this afternoon,

Dear," she replies.

Whew! I think to myself. Now I can get back to all those wonderful things I have been waiting until retirement to do. My biggest problem is I can't seem to recall what was so exciting about retirement a few years ago, before it actually happened. I guess if I were to be totally honest with myself, I never really expected to retire, willingly or otherwise. Hell, I never expected to reach fifty, not the way I was burning the candle at both ends and three places in the middle. But here I am, trying to make the best of the situation and doing a fairly decent job of it. I have the opportunity to go to ball games, to read and write and to goof off, to work a little and play a little and go a little. Not bad, heh? Still . . . .

About this point in my daydreaming, my fishing buddy shows up on the pretense of using the phone or bringing by some donuts or whatever. FishBud always has some kind of a story to tell before he ever rings the doorbell. Generally, it's "I heard the fish were really biting again up at the dam last week." It's usually last week when the big ones either got away or were caught by some mysterious stranger who took his fish and vanished into some sort of etheric twilight zone. When we do go out fishing, we always seem to be either a week late or a week early or on the wrong river. It's downright uncanny how that seems to work. But still, I do enjoy getting out amongst'em.

"You know you're getting older when . . .

. . . you need a morning checklist to make sure all your body parts are in proper functioning order. That's just one example of a "Senior Moment."

. . . your appointment calendar has pages and pages of empty.

AM CHECKLIST

_____ Blood pumping

_____ Lungs breathing

_____ Limbs moving

_____ Eyes open; glasses

_____ Dentures in

_____ Bladder drained

_____ Bowels moved

_____ Brain engaged

_____ Voice in tune

_____ Mouth in gear

_____ "Good Morning!"

You know you're getting older when . . .

. . . there are two signs of advancing age. The first is the loss of memory, and I forgot the other one. (Maybe it was to use a checklist).

TWO

Healthcare

I rarely took pills before I became an *Honored Citizen*. I remember taking an aspirin for a mild headache once about fifteen years ago. Now my Primary Healthcare Provider has me taking pills for high blood pressure, acid reflux, allergies, an aspirin a day for a healthy heart and an assortment of pills and medicines that would choke the healthiest of horses.

It seems to me that you can't go to a doctor any more without him or her prescribing another armful of pills and potions. Primary Healthcare Provider says he is responsible for my well-being. I wonder if he is so almighty responsible, will he take my place when it comes time for me to leave this world. Whatever happened to "Here now, you just rest easy and let me take that thorn out of your paw."

I have developed a theory that Primary Healthcare Providers are required to take a simple course before they are released from medical school and turned loose on the general public. The course is given

during medical school and is called "I am God 101." This course establishes an attitude that will carry doctors through their entire medical careers. It completely seals the god-like attitude into their brains and closes off any possibilities for further discussion regarding a patient's concept of what troubles him. Consequently, we now have the "ailment of the month." Regardless of what the patient experiences as a symptom, Primary Healthcare Provider is going to prescribe a very expensive dose of the very latest "Drug Manufacturer Deal of the Month." Now I'm not suggesting that Primary Healthcare Provider and Drug Manufacturer are in each other's pockets but why should I pay top dollar to get a prescription for something that doesn't begin to address my latest aches and pains?

And while we are on the topic of Drug Manufacturers, do not for one moment believe that Drug Manufacturers give one hoot in hell if I live or die. Oh, I know they make all this noise about being concerned about the health and well-being of the world populace. But when the cameras aren't running, the stockholders have their eyes firmly fixed on the "bottom line." What I don't understand is why drug manufacturers spend so much money on advertising prescription drugs on television and in magazines.

Reportedly, prescription drug reactions have escalated to become the number four cause of death in this country, behind heart attacks, cancer and strokes. Adverse drug reactions to prescriptions now kill about the same number of people each year as car accidents. These reports don't do a whole lot for my confidence in the drug industry.

No, I have decided that the only person in the world to look out for my health and well-being has to be me. Admittedly, WifeBud shows a lot of concern and is always there if I need her. Sometimes she even hovers over me so well that I occasionally call her Helicopter. Still, she has to guard her own H&WB.

Recently, WifeBud and I went to see Medical Doctor turned Nutritionist. This would not even be worthy of a mention except for a couple of interesting facts. First of all, the god of all gods, the Medical Establishment, must surely consider an MD turned Nutritionist, who recommends vitamins and health supplements, as the ultimate of all traitors. Secondly, I did not bother to mention to Primary Healthcare Provider that I was getting medical advice outside his godhood. But remember, Primary Healthcare Provider, who claims total responsibility for my health and well-being has declined to stand in for me when Gabriel blows his horn in my direction. Maybe I'm trying to hedge my bet a little with this alternative stuff but why not join the rest of the anxious crowd. If Primary Healthcare Provider says it's useless, then what's the harm; it only costs money. Besides, all those health food supplements make me feel so self-righteous when I take them by the handful every morning, noon and night.

The only problem with all these pills and potions is when WifeBud and I travel. We decided to separate the prescriptions, vitamins and supplements into little envelopes of doses by the time of day when it is to be consumed. Since I take this "stuff" (a technical term for health paraphernalia) at four different times of day and WifeBud takes hers three times a day, we have a total of seven little envelopes a day for each day we travel. This is also good for the paper envelope economy, so everyone wins. The fun part is trying to manhandle all those slippery little envelopes while trying to keep them in some sort of order. Otherwise, when we are driving and stop for lunch we have all these envelopes that we have to sort through, looking for times and dates, with rubber bands breaking and envelopes flying. It gets a bit awkward in public.

While on the subject of health care in general, I would like to express my feelings about hospitals. This is the place where the gods of the Medical Establishment congregate to decide who lives, who dies and who gets tormented beyond what is normally considered reasonable human endurance. The only saving grace in hospitals is the nurses, without whom the average senior patient would probably just as soon cash it all in.

Recently, I had an opportunity to visit a hospital. My boating buddy had suffered a small stroke and I went to visit him. BoatBud's Medical Provider had the bedside manner of a grizzly bear with a sore behind. He tore into BoatBud, and every other person within ear shot about their smoking habits. Perhaps Medical Provider figured the only way to get BoatBud's attention was to go ballistic. He may have been right; however, I believe even the gods should try to act in a civilized manner when in a healing institution and environment. I really thought

some of the other patients on that floor were going to go screaming out of the building in their open-in-the-back bed gowns, dragging their IV stands and tubes behind them.

Another interesting thing about some Medical Types is that they occasionally go beyond diagnosis and set themselves up as Judge and Jury with a verdict. I remember a number of years ago when a young doctor came walking into an occupied waiting room and about halfway across the room, said loud enough for all to hear, "Well, you only have about three months to live." This highly educated nitwit took on the role of Judge, Jury and Executioner, but maybe gods are allowed to do that -- *I don't think so.*

Anyhow, at about the same time BoatBud was getting his derriere thoroughly remodeled by his Primary Medical Provider, my Daughter was in another hospital many miles away giving birth to a new grandson. A hospital can be good for some and unfortunate for others. This causes me to have a very mixed attitude about hospitals, namely, let somebody else be their paying guests. However, it's sure nice to know they are available in a pinch. Been there, done that. More than once.

"You know you're getting older when . . .

. . . you're on a first name basis with an internist, an allergist, a dermatologist, a gastroenterologist, a cardiologist, and an audiologist. (Your first name, not theirs -- you don't get too familiar with the gods).

. . . your medications come in childproof bottles and you have to get the little kid next door to open them.

. . . you enrich your vocabulary with firsthand knowledge of such interesting new words as "osteoarthritis, carotid endarterectomy, angiogram, esophogoscopy."

. . . you remember that at one time you could eat anything on the menu without a problem. And castor oil would cure anything.

. . . the majority of your monthly income is spent on either HMO insurance or on vitamins and supplements or both.

23

"You know you're getting older when . . .

. . . you can't remember if the doctor said, "Take one every four hours and call me when they are gone or take four every hour and call the hospital in the morning."

. . . a person is cautioned to slow down by a doctor instead of the police.

. . . you subscribe to yet another health magazine or newsletter.

THREE

The sky is falling, the sky is falling

For as long as I can remember, and this must be a philosophical, economic or Karmic law of some sort, there has always been some pseudo-authoritarian screwball who considers it his mission in life to stir up the squirrels in the population. Some people cannot handle living in a world of peace and harmony; periodically they have to stir the pot.

I first became truly aware of this truism when my schoolteacher bride came home one day toward the end of a school year. She reported that the school district had announced that it had run out of funds; there were going to be teacher layoffs before the beginning of the following year. This was a matter of great concern for a dedicated, lifelong professional teacher of third and fourth grade little rugrats. She had not taken into account her many years of seniority and service to the community, when she let herself become so upset. This announcement had served its purpose of getting the entire district teaching staff in a total frenzy. Basically, it got the weak and marginal teachers to look for positions elsewhere, which was also good for McDonald's staffing concerns.

Those who decided to "wait it out" were left hanging until the eleventh hour. Then someone decided to ask if the administrative work force would be affected by the downsizing. It was then discovered that there was one administrative type for every three classroom teachers. To say this school system was a top heavy organization would have been a gross understatement in anyone's vocabulary. It's also very fascinating how the top district officials suddenly and "miraculously" found "just enough" funds to keep the schools open for "another year" with the remaining staff.

Now, this "chicken little" type of administrative management does not stop at just a local school district level; it pervades all levels of government. One year, a county board of supervisors decided to surreptitiously give themselves a huge raise in salary. They knew they couldn't raise taxes again, so they decided to cut back on some services. They started by cutting back on library services and high school sports programs. One of the surer ways of bringing out the "squirrels looking for nuts" is to curtail library hours and services or try to do without high school football. This will inspire all the intellectual types to paint all manner of placards and

march on city hall. All the sports nuts will gather at the local stadium in uniform, with banners and pompoms to display their displeasure at this latest affront to sensibility. In the end, after much posturing and negotiating, the fans of sports and libraries finally agree to a "small" tax increase. The politicos add a hidden addendum to the agreement giving themselves a fat salary "adjustment" and everyone walks away feeling they have won something.

This concept works equally well on a national level. Case in point -- we have to have a balanced federal budget; the country can't possibly survive without a balanced budget amendment. The sky is falling, heaven help us, the sky is falling. The national debt is off the scale of reality. By another "miraculous event," our Glorious Leader did a little creative accounting, and saints be praised, we have a balanced budget. Now all we have to do is worry about Social Security going broke by the year 2032. Somebody has got to take up the banner! Where are all those squirrels that run around gathering nuts, just when you need them?

Now if you stop for just a moment and do the math, most of the seniors now over 65 are not terribly likely to be in this world in the year 2032. Those Baby Boomers who are approaching the Golden Age are the ones that currently hold the purse strings of the government. So, do you think for one minute they are going to let the politicians give away the Golden Goose without digging out their old placards and banners and doing some serious marching? Not on your old pompom, my friends. There will be the usual crowds of "squirrels running around looking for nuts" that are determined to keep the sky from falling, well, at least not permanently. And you know what? They will succeed, once again, in keeping the sky in exactly the right place, shape and altitude, thank you very much.

."You know you're getting older when . . .

. . . you see books written by Dave Barry and Bill Geist about turning fifty and you wonder what do those young, Baby Boomer squirts know about aging. Oh, to be fifty again.

. . . Doctors, lawyers and police officers all look like refugees from playpens, and you unwittingly address them as "Young Fellow" or "Young Lady."

FOUR

Getting there

Contrary to some beliefs, and I will not mention names (Progeny), I was not born as a senior citizen. I was born and became a father at a very early age (huh?). To date, I have not had some young squirt ask me my secret of longevity, but I know it's coming sooner rather than later. So to avoid the rush for knowledge, I would like to give my opinion now. But first I want you to know that I have done an in-depth study of this subject. I remember my great-grand-mother and her four daughters, my great-aunts, very well, and I learned from them. Then I confirmed my newly acquired knowledge by checking it against other models of seniority.

The essence of this wisdom can be stated in one word - THINK. Now don't let the simplicity of that statement lead you into a false sense of hope. I know young people right now, that for all intents and purposes, could be considered by some folks to be brain dead. Oh, their bodies still move quite well and are often the envy of many seniors, but when asked a serious question, the eyes often go blank and it becomes obvious that the brain has slipped into neutral. If you are the least bit sensitive, you can even detect this condition when you are on the phone.

For example, suppose you call a large corporation looking for some simple product information. First of all, this corporation can't find a reliable employee with enough intelligence to come in out of the rain, who can answer the phones sensibly, so you are directed to use a telephone push button menu. These menus can rattle on indefinitely, played in fast forward so they are almost impossible to understand, without ever mentioning anything close to the department you want to contact. If you are fortunate enough to get through to the right department extension at all, more often than not you will be put on hold long enough that you will wish you had brought a picnic lunch. Then there is that marvel of modern technology, voice mail - "Please leave your name and phone number and we will get back to you before your 93rd birthday or a year from Wednesday, whichever comes latest." Hey, I'm already a senior citizen and just want a simple question answered, okay?

Finally, the day arrives and you get a return call. Your question has lost a lot of its impact since you originally made the request for information, but you figure they were kind enough to call back, finally, so you will ask anyhow. Now these young people are trained to think in "parameters," an interesting word that means "everything I am able to discuss has to fit into this small, two-dimensional box of information on my computer screen or you will overload my brain and I could blow a cerebral circuit breaker." This person has a real good handle on about three minutes of pretty serious sounding technibabble and then starts repeating himself verbatim. However, his little computer screen gives him absolutely no indication that he is at any time supposed to have a thought outside his parameter. Independent thought is mightily frowned upon and can even be grounds for dismissal. "Thank you very kindly for the call, you were very helpful and I've learned a lot, let's do it again some time," I'm saying, trying to get off the phone before he starts the techni-babble tape over again from the beginning.

Now consider this for a moment. If our friendly corporate techni-twit cannot think for himself while representing his company, what is going to happen when the 5 o'clock whistle blows and he is turned loose on the

freeway in his oversize monster truck, hiding behind tinted windows, boom box blaring, with a beer in one hand and a cell phone in the other hand, tailgating any driver unfortunate enough to get caught in front of him, totally oblivious to the siren and flashing lights of the emergency vehicle behind him. It's Friday night and he's in one helluva hurry to get home and prop up his feet on the coffee table, pop open another beer and plan a weekend of recreation. Recreation, in this case, means pushing something to its ultimate limit.

This limit can take any number of forms: skydiving, rock-face cliff climbing, off-trail snow boarding, car racing on and off the track, bungee jumping, and on and on -- as long as it can be considered as "pushing the limits." It has to have a major adrenaline rush. Throttle to the firewall, pedal to the metal, and the devil can take the hindmost; our intrepid adventurer is infallible and will live forever -- or so it seems, if television sitcoms are any indication. Operating with an attitude like that can get a person very seriously and permanently dead. So much for becoming just another senior citizen.

Even if our adventurer survives, he will likely have to be rescued by people who are willing to risk life and limb to save him. Then he will gather a team of attorneys and sue the mountain or the lake or whomever he thinks is responsible for his plight.

As I mentioned at the top of this section, I was not born a senior citizen; I really did have a childhood. I even did some pretty dumb things as a growing boy and young man. Lots of dumbs. As a teenager, I remember talking FirstLove into swimming across the lake one fine afternoon. I'm extremely lucky that two families weren't put through a horrible grieving process as two young bodies were grappled off the bottom of the lake. Or risking life and limb with FirstLove on one of the few rare occasions when I was allowed to use the family car, not from speed, just doing dumb things. Then much later, I decided I had to give up trying to be the great wild game hunter because I would probably wind up having an apple stuffed in my mouth because of some dumb mistake. When I was about 42 years old, I learned how to fly small single engine airplanes. A life long dream. It was about then that I decided that I could no longer afford dumb mistakes, especially thousands of feet above terra firma. No point at all in making the top of the evening news -- "Dumb pilot does a dumb."

In spite of all the dumb things I did manage to create and escape, it never once occurred to me to purposely "push the limit, live on the edge, get the adrenaline pumping." That may make me a chicken by today's standards, and that's okay, because I am still a living, breathing, thinking senior chicken, thank you very much.

Mistakes are one way we learn, and learning is critical and it takes some thinking to learn. It's when we don't think and/or consider consequences that we get into serious trouble. Senior citizens are short on trouble and long on thinking and surviving. They realize just how precious life can be. They also realize that it does not go on forever, not in this form at least.

You know you're getting older when . . .

. . . you finally know all the answers, but nobody asks the questions any more.

FIVE

Games seniors play

"After all I've done for you. Didn't I give you birth and wipe your butt and feed you at my very breast and take care of you, and this is the way you treat me. You haven't called me in three hours. How can you live with yourself?"

"Yes, Ma." The words change from time to time, but the implication is always the same; I took care of you (whether you wanted it or not) and now it's your turn to take care of me. Never mind that I left home when I was nineteen years old and that I am now a senior citizen in my own right. In her mind, her nineteen years of toil and sacrifice and pain have entitled her to almost fifty years of my life as repayment of a never-ending debt. It took me most of those fifty years to get her to understand that I was old enough to wear long pants, which was a sure sign that her little boy was growing up.

Just perhaps, almost maybe, I have been a little hard on my own children. I am still of the opinion that I have lived longer and I might know something that they  haven't learned just yet. FirstBorn decided long ago that I had missed my calling and should have been a preacher. When I call him on the phone, his first question is often, "What's today's sermon, Dad?" Or, "No sermon this time? Are you feeling okay,

"The Sermonizer"

Dad?" SecondBorn just kind of ignores the whole idea and does her own thing, whatever that means.

Games with one's SoulMate can be fun, too. "While you're up" is one of the easiest games to get drawn into. "While you're up, would you please get me another drink from the fridge?" It always pays to be polite when you are playing this game. Or she will say, "While you're up, would you please hand me that dish from the topshelf of the cabinet?" Some times this game can get

40

really ridiculous when one person purposely delays hoisting it out of an easy chair because they know a "While you're up" will be requested and all you want to do is make a quick trip to that little room with the indoor plumbing. Generally, it's all good-natured fun as long as both parties are aware of what is happening.

WifeBud loves the "Coupon Game." You can see this game being played by many seniors at the supermarkets. They all start with forty thousand little pieces of paper that offer 10¢ off the purchase price of a particular product and brand name. The object of the game is to match the coupon with the product, by brand name, with the coupon expiration date. It's extra points if you have coupons for something you're even interested in buying. Getting to the check-out register, with the appropriate coupons, without dropping half of them while writing a check gets to be the real trick.

Some of these games can get more than just a little silly. One of the first to come to mind is the "I got mine" game. This situation generally has to do with controlling population growth and where or where not the opposition can build housing for said growing population. Case in point. One of my favorite places in the whole world is the Mendocino Coast of California. One weekend when we were just visiting the area, some of the no-growth advocates were having a rally and march protesting any further development of the general area. One of these well-intended young people was struggling to get her large sign placard out of her car, then she proceeded to eject two small children from the car. It was at this point that I noticed that she was obviously very pregnant. Then I saw that she had New York license plates on her car and couldn't help but consider the incongruity of this scene; she was from out of state but probably felt "I've got mine, lock the gates." Then I wondered about her children; there is no space for them in her plan. What's she going to do when they reach child-bearing age, take'em out and drown'em? I certainly hope not.

I have seen the "I've got mine" game played just as fervently by senior citizens with children and grand-children. "We don't want any more homes built in this county." They obviously want their offspring to live in

somebody else's county, where they aren't wanted either. I saw this happen in a predominately rural county with only one town of any noteworthy size, and it had less than 15,000 residents. There was no growth and no jobs for young people, so they left, in droves. The local joke was that the last young person to leave town was to turn out the lights. James Dillet Freeman may have said it best, "When you're green you grow, when you're ripe you rot." So much for no growth, senior or otherwise.

A variation of the "I've got mine" game is called Nimby -- Not in my back yard. We all want our lives to be as Utopian as possible. We also want all the creature comforts available. Want a good job? Build a clean factory in someone else's area, not in my back yard. Want a glass of milk? Keep those dirty, smelly cows some-where else, not in my back yard. Want freedom from crime? Yes, but place the jails far, far away. Want culture and entertainment? Yes, but I don't want them too close -- I don't want to see them or hear them except when I go to them. And if my neighbor likes that sort of thing, that's his problem, just don't put them in my back yard. Want convenient shopping? Yes, but not too close -- all that traffic is disturbing my serenity.

On the flip side of this "no growth" coin are the vast ideas for wonderfulness (read as "wild money making opportunities") with half-vast plans and no consideration for the population in general and the environment in par-ticular. I find it most interesting how some groups can push and shove the most inane plans imaginable. I have seen voters reject an idea just to have some political or big money type continue trying to promote a pet project. The attitude seems to be that if you have enough money or see yourself as the "big frog" in a little pond, you should be allowed to have your way, regardless of how ill-conceived the plan may happen to be.

I feel seniors have a responsibility to act as the protectors of the progeny, the caretakers of the careless, the custodians of the citizenry and the guardians of the future. Take up the cause! Raise the banners! March to the pipe and the drum! Forward Ho! (Who was that masked man?)

And the games go on.

You know you're getting older when . . .

. . . you would be happy to put things back where they belong if you could just remember where that was.

. . . you don't worry about avoiding temptation. At your age it will avoid you.

. . . it's great fun to read the Sunday newspaper list of celebrity birthdays until you realize those "older folks" you always looked up to are actually younger than you.

SIX

Let's have a get-together

The very mention of anything that sounds like a reunion is enough to make some of us go looking for a place to hide. In my view, family reunions are events put together by some of the ladies for the sole purpose of exchanging gossip and making unwarranted comparisons.

What man in his right mind would want to attend a family reunion? The faces never seem to change, there's only more of them. Family members grow up, get married and produce more family members. The numbers keep growing, just like a bunch of rabbits. Then there are divorces and remarriages with his kids, her kids and their kid in the oven. It becomes almost impossible to determine who belongs to whom. And all those young offspring are just a collection of runny noses and wet,

smelly undergarments adorned on dirty little faces trying to get a chance to sit on your lap and beg for candy.
"Hey, I'm not your Pied Piper. Isn't that your mother I

hear calling you?" The neat thing about being a senior
is you can love'em and spoil'em and then send'em back
to their mommas.

Then there is always an UncleBlowHard who can't wait to tell everyone, individually or in groups, what a wonderful buy he made on that acreage on the other side of the county. He and his half-brother KnowItAll made the deal of a lifetime on that property and with just a few investors putting up a few thousand dollars each, "and we're going to give you first shot at it, we will subdivide that property into two acre parcels and we'll clean up." What they don't know, and I don't want to burst their bubble, is that "clean up" are the key words here -- that property has just been determined to be a toxic waste dump and it will take massive dollars and decades before those new condemned signs are taken down.

We wouldn't want to forget cousin OneUpmanShip. No matter what anyone else has ever done, he's done it faster, longer, bigger, slower, more intently, more expensively, less expensively, bolder, cooler and with more savior-faire than anyone that has ever lived during the past century and a half. This obviously qualifies him to be God's personal gift to women. Speaking of which, his current wife, Miss SexSymbol 1964 is the primary role model for ninety-two percent of all dumb blonde jokes. Yes, they are a happily married, fun loving couple -- at least in public.

Miss PennyPincher is bound to be at any function that will get her out in public where she can be noticed. In a restaurant she will invariably make several of those loud, squeaky-voiced complaints about the food, the service, the decor and anything else that catches her attention. After the meal, when the check finally arrives, the rest of us just want to pay the bill and fade quietly away into the sunset. PennyPincher turns into the auditor from hell who wants every cent accounted for and everyone has to pay his or her own portion, no exceptions. "And how dare they charge so much for such food and service." It only takes one of these, never to be repeated, episodes to ruin any pleasant concerns you may have ever had for her. You know at any repeat performance, you will cheerfully and instantly be arrested, tried and immediately convicted of manslaughter.

Most family reunions also have a DaddyGotRocks. He's the old guy that a few of the younger women make a big deal of making sure he knows how proud they are to be in his will, whether they really are or not. They also make sure they manipulate themselves into a favorable position so he gets a nice long look at a lot of cleavage, real or artificially endowed. And he isn't missing a thing, especially any mental faculties.

The lady-folk all have a good gossip about who's sleeping with whom and how well he takes care of his sleeping duties and functions. And whose husband just bought a new off-road sport utility vehicle, and who lost his/her job, and who moved into that old brown house over on the east side of town, and isn't it too bad that the SocialClimber side of the family doesn't associate any more than necessary with this side of the family because we don't shop at Hoity-Toity Emporium. I guess it's a good chance for the lady folk to recharge their conversational skills and gossip batteries. I suppose this behavior is basically harmless but it's all so predictable.

School reunions are pretty much the same type of situation with a couple of notable differences. Economic differences are now more apparent. You will often hear comments spoken in very soft voices, "Look where I would be now if I had married that one." This is a statement that has both positive and negative connotations, depending on whom the speaker is referring to.

For the men, it's an opportunity to check out the ones that were the "babes" of days gone by. You find out that the one that you thought was so fast and loose with every guy in school but you, and really wasn't, is now Mother Superior in some far off convent. The gal that was so unapproachable in school now has a dozen or so kids and would make a model poster for the Pope's views on birth control.

There's the jock of the year sitting alone over in the corner. His hair seems to be resting slightly side-saddle and it's obviously a cheap toupee. He looks like something the cat dragged in and then decided to reject. He certainly doesn't look very healthy. I guess steroids can only keep the body going for just a limited time.

Our lovely homecoming queen is still quite attractive after all these years and three husbands. Too bad she never really made it big as a super model or dancer. She runs a small dance school in the old part of downtown. Nice legs.

As the years and the reunions drag on, senior citizens generally go to these functions to find out who has survived this long. "What ever happened to good old WhatsHisName? Oh, you know the one I mean, had all that hair and a dimple, right in the middle of, and used to ride a, that funny thing, and lived over, oh, you know who I mean, don't you?" Not a clue. Memories all too often get distorted out of anything even beginning to resemble true past history. "You and I had a fight and have not been on speaking terms for years? How could that be? I always remembered us as being best of friends. Oh, I didn't remember that part. I am sorry but you surely must see how funny it all seems now. Oh, you still don't think so." And life, and the years, go on, and on.

I've never been to a military reunion. My military experience was not all that dramatic or noteworthy. Still, I would imagine it's about who has survived this long and paying homage to those that are no longer present. I guess I feel that it's not terribly polite to call upon old ghosts just so I can feel better for the tribute. But like I said; I've never been there. Quick, somebody play Taps (before I get in any deeper).

And then let's pay tribute to the living!

SEVEN

Exercise and fitness

"Seniors need to get more exercise." "Seniors should be more aware of physical fitness." "To live a long and fulfilling life, you must move dem bones." You gotta do this, quit doing that, move, move, move! In case you haven't noticed, I'm older than most of those young squirts making all those demands on my body.

I have always exercised -- even three to five times a day. For years my daily exercise regimen has consisted of elbow bends, arm raises and wrist turns, generally with metal objects in my hands, more specifically, a knife and a fork. I also do walking, so much so in fact that I have a well-worn path between my easy chair and the dinner table. Just these two particular sets of exercises have kept me going for a very long time and I'm sure I would have wasted away to nothing without them.

I even get regular physical checkups. Well, maybe regular is not the best word; occasional might be more appropriate. Physical exams are not my favorite way to spend a morning. I can get by without my morning caffeine fix for a couple of hours and I can even pee in a bottle on cue. However, I really don't care much for this vampire routine. My blood veins went into seclusion

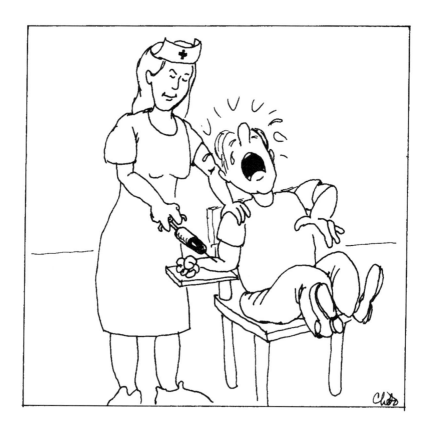

years ago and have been in hiding ever since. Finding a draw spot is a real trick that I don't care to have performed very often.

Still, I manage to handle all this checkup routine with a certain amount of emotional detachment. That is until Primary Health Provider pulls on a pair of rubber gloves. It is at this point that I involuntarily tighten every voluntary muscle in my body. Talk about buns of steel! And when he says to bend over onto the examining table, my back goes ramrod straight and my legs turn into the Pillars of Hercules. "Relax," he says. "You're too tense," he says. "You need to exercise more," he says.

Recently WifeSoulMateBud and I started an exercise program for seniors at one of the local health club/gyms. This is a forty-five minute workout led by Sweet Young Thing. Most of these exercises are accomplished while seated. At one time I would have thought this was the most ridiculous situation imaginable but SYT knows what she is doing --getting a bunch of old fuddy-duddies to stretch a muscle or two.

I have seen some seniors go totally bizarre on exercise and fitness. Those are the ones that run up the side of Oregon's 11,239 ft. Mt. Hood and never huff a single puff. I huff and puff just pulling my pants on. Some of those folks just like to make the rest of us feel envious -- and you know what? -- they succeeded.

Moderation -- that's my motto -- moderation in all things. Back to my elbow bends, arm raises and wrist turn exercises. Moderation. Would you please pass the biscuits and gravy?

You know you're getting older when . . .

. . . you realize that caution is the only thing you really care to exercise.

. . . your mind makes contracts your body can't keep.

. . . adjusting your head so you can see through your bifocals is the only exercise your neck ever gets.

. . . work is a lot less work and fun is a lot more work.

. . . you become paranoid about receiving junk mail from nursing homes or the local undertaker.

. . . you discover you can purchase clothes that actually fit from the "Portly" section of the men's clothing store.

. . . it takes longer to rest than it did to get tired.

. . . your knees buckle and your belt won't.

EIGHT

On the brighter side

"Some day I'm going to retire and sleep until noon every day. No more of this getting up at the crack of dawn and trudging off to work. No more time clocks; no more management meetings or three martini lunches or whatever." It's like the World War II comedy song, "Some Day I'm Going to Murder the Bugler." We come up with all of these lovely ideas, but when the day of opportunity arrives, the realization is not nearly as sweet as the anticipation. What was once thought to be a wonderful idea, this forbidden fruit, has suddenly lost its appeal. Many senior citizens must reinvent their desires and establish new priorities.

Travel is probably one of the most desirable activities for newly-hatched senior retirees. The good news is that there are abundant opportunities for discounts on travel packages for seniors. Airlines, hotels, motels, tourist attractions, restaurants, movie theaters and many other activities offer discounts to seniors. Sometimes you have to ask or search out these discounts. The downside news is that even discounted, travel can get expensive after a while. It's easy to run out of money long before you run out of exciting places to visit. Then there's all that wear and tear on the old bod when traveling, but it surely is fun at times.

It would seem that everyone's grandchildren are scattered to the winds. This is especially true for those families that have been involved in divorces and re-marriages. This does give seniors an opportunity to climb into their motor homes and travel-trailers and join the masses on the highways. Getting some of these underpowered behemoths up steep hills can be a real trick. An even bigger trick is to keep your cool when you are stuck behind one of these monsters that is trying to get up the hill.

When WifeBud is stuck behind one of these vehicles, she tells everyone following her that "it's not my fault

for the slow traffic" (as if they could hear her) and she proceeds to enjoy the scenery. I do enjoy the bumper snickers, especially the one stating "We're spending our children's inheritance." Good for you.

There are a lot of less expensive alternatives to constant travel which can be found in most towns and cities. Good places to start are the local senior center, the parks and recreation department, a junior college or other learning institution. There are all sorts of interesting activities that catch a person's attention. These can lead to developing new friendships, interests, hobbies and/or avocations.

Many health clubs now have special programs which can be a lot of fun for seniors. Most cities have a library, which can be a great source of pleasure as well as exercising the think tank. Most of these are not designed for the chronic couch potato, so you may have to get off your butt and on your feet. You could start a business or two, not to compete with General Motors or AT &T, just small stuff, like a bookkeeping service or desktop publishing or a woodshop building birds' nests, or whatever strikes your fancy. I find it very stimulating to have three or four irons in the fire at any given moment.

I still haven't struck a chord yet? Volunteer. There are dozens of people and places nearby that look for volunteers: hospitals, schools, libraries, churches and if you can't find one, you're not looking. Try volunteering in an elementary school classroom and see what our teachers have to cope with each day -- you will hear playground language the likes of which I never experienced in my military career.

The Internet is a source of pleasure for a lot of seniors; however, I'm also hearing about a lot of people who have maxed out on it. After a person has surfed the net for a gazillion hours, what else is there? Diversify. It makes sense. Have a lot of varied interests. Even most golf nuts don't spend all their waking hours on the course. Try something different, even sex -- participating, or fantasizing or both, depending on your Viagra supply.

You know you're getting older when ...

... sex is only something discussed at great length on television, but you don't find any of the jokes even amusing.

... your pacemaker makes the garage door go up when you see a pretty girl walk by, but that's all that goes up.

... you forgot if you took a nap this afternoon, so you sit down for just a minute or two to rest your eyes.

NINE

Crotchety old men

Sometimes it is difficult for men to express in civil terms what they mean to one another. Case in point: BoatBud had a mild stroke recently. BoatBud has always been active and does not like restrictions. BoatBud's mind is as sharp (or dull -- just kidding) as ever, although BoatBud does not articulate all that well now. He says he can think it properly, but has trouble saying it right. BoatBud thinks he should be able to drive any of his many vehicles, with an over-sized pickup as the weapon of choice.

BoatBud has been married to a nice lady for almost fifty years. NiceLady tries to reason with him, but BoatBud has heard it all before -- especially from her, and generally goes his merry way.

Enter YoursTruly, me, into this scene. Now, I think

the world of BoatBud. I also know he can be one hard-headed individual. I know this because we are so much alike. We even share the same birthday.

Now when BoatBud wants to do something that I think is stupid, and/or dangerous, I take it upon myself to call it to BoatBud's attention. This makes me somewhat of a crotchety old man (as opposed to grumpy).

My dictionary defines "crotchety" as "given to odd fancies or whims; eccentric." The secondary definitions refer to "grouchy or cantankerous." In this case, I prefer whims or eccentric because it allows for caring, respect, concern and affection.

If I can save BoatBud from doing a dumb, I'm going to be right in the middle of it. Unfortunately, I tend to get a little emotional and occasionally let my temper get the best of the situation. As an example, recently BoatBud decided he wanted to make the twelve mile trip into town. There was snow and ice on the roads and the public was advised to stay home unless there was a critical need. BoatBud decided this particular trip to town was a "life or death matter" for him, and he proceeded to involve everyone he knew into this mess. He couldn't convince me it was all that important, so I proceeded to let him know, in no uncertain terms, what I thought of his needs and desires. In this case, BoatBud didn't take too kindly to my ranting and raving, regardless of my caring and concern, even if I couldn't express it in a rational manner; yea, me, the great communicator. That's what some crotchety old guys do on occasion: show caring and concern in weird ways.

Part of this crotchety behavior probably stems from the idea that some of us feel we have seen it all, and done most of it, which we feel qualifies us to tell others how to, or how not to behave. And the greater the concern or age difference, the more intense the teaching or the telling.

Sometimes this doesn't work especially well with the younger generation. "But Dad," whines Progeny, "I want to do it myself, I want to be able to make my own mistakes."

Give me strength, Lord. What do I have to do to get these young people to listen to good sense?

"Would you just listen for a moment?" I say. "One of the major differences between people and puppy dogs, besides the number and the function of legs involved, is the ability of people to learn from their mistakes and pass that knowledge on to their offspring. Puppy dogs can't do that."

Now that's a pretty convincing, logical explanation of how things work. I felt that bit of wisdom should have put me right up there with the greatest philosophical minds: Socrates, Aristotle, Plato, Yogi Berra, et al. Hah! Oh how we intellectuals can delude ourselves, especially when it comes to our offspring, and even more so when we are talking about their offspring.

Grand-progeny has been driving automobiles for probably six years now. During that time he has managed to do a three-roll crash in his dad's brand new van and generally demolish a various assortment of other vehicles, including another of his dad's cars. This young person is either a one-man demolition derby or aspiring to be a test car crash-dummy.

"Ya know, I don't see what the big deal is, ya know. Everybody's bugging out over nothing, ya know. And it's not like I'm hurting anybody else, ya know." Duh.

I got my first driver's license over fifty years ago. To this date, I have never been in an automobile accident. That doesn't make me right and the young squirt wrong. It just shows a little more concern for life, limb and the value of property.

I have tried to gently pass on to my grand-progeny some of the lessons that I have learned over the years. Sixty-something-plus years of living, many of which have been in the world of business, should give me some background to make a few minor recommendations for the fine art of living in today's world. But such is not considered to be the case.

So many of today's youngsters are instant authorities on any subject you can name. If it's in the English language, they know more about it than anyone, especially crotchety old men. I am beginning to learn that Papas and Grandpas are to be pitied and tolerated. We are considered to be hopelessly old-fashioned and out of date in the eyes of this younger generation. Too bad too, we have so much we could share if we could just get someone to listen.

One of my major goals in life has developed into a desire to live long enough and learn enough to be as smart as some of my grand-progeny profess to be. I don't suppose it will be until they have joined the ranks of

Honored Citizens that they will realize they weren't so damned smart after all. I'm sure it took me about that long.

You know you're getting older when . . .

. . . you finally know all the answers, but nobody asks the questions any more.

. . . you feel like you're a perfect living example of "Too soon old, too late smart."

You know you're getting older when . . .

. . . your first two grandsons are larger than you, still live with their parents and don't know for sure if you're a great-grandpa or not.

. . . your favorite part of the newspaper is the "50 years ago today" column.

TEN

Those good old days

As people grow older, they collect more memories. (How's that for a profound statement?). My point is that some of us folks have seen a lot, done a lot, and learned a lot along the way. Some of the younger folks would say "So What," without realizing they might learn something or that they might be stomping on someone's personal history. Still, it's fun to reminisce a little now and again.

Cars are a great source of memories of the good old days. I can still remember the days of blow-outs and dozens of patches on tubes in tires. Hand-crank starters that could kick like the wildest mule. Even wheels that would fall off moving cars at the most inconvenient times and places; like you are driving across a bridge in a hurry to get some place and a wheel goes flying off into the bay. And Ford Motor Company saying you could have a car of any color you liked -- as long as it was black.

When I hear people complaining about the lack of an air conditioner or CD player in their cars, I can remember back to the time when cars didn't even have car heaters. Three of us siblings sat in the back seat of the family car, huddled under a blanket, trying to keep from freezing to death on a cold night. Being the oldest of the three, I felt it was my right and privilege to sit in the middle where it was warmest, while the other two would huddle up to big brother. RHIP! Rank Has It's Privileges, I say. Of course, in the summer, rank and privilege decreed that I should have the best window seat.

Those old cars of my early youth were great adventure-mobiles. I was a teenager before our family ever had a vehicle that even had a radio in it. So those were the days of "imagination." From the preferred window seat, every cloud had a formation that looked like an animal or a person or something equally fascinating. Every forest was the secret hideout of Robin Hood or the place where the cavalry or the army of the good guys watched and prepared to attack the bad guys that were in the adjoining meadow. And just over the next hill would be a city of tall glass buildings with airplanes flying everywhere. I loved airplanes, real or imagined. Still do. Imagination, what a wonderful gift to be given by the Creator -- and now you can get a TV built into some of today's vehicles; what a terrible waste of brain power.

One of the things that I particularly remember learning the hard way was respect for my elders. When I was in the growing up stages, I picked myself up off the floor more than once when I forgot to show respect for my elders, which were any of those folks who were adults, especially related adults. "Yes sir, no ma'am, please and thank you."

Today's youth have no such respect (youth being anyone less than 45 years old). One of the expressions used by today's youth that I find particularly annoying is "you guys." WifeBud and I will be in a restaurant and a very young waitperson will say, "So what do *you guys* want to order?" I am not a *'you guy'*! And I don't consider 'you guy'as being very respectful. Unfortunately, it's in fairly common usage these days - and worse yet, I find myself using it occasionally.

School teachers of my time were some of the most respected individuals anywhere. Their job was to teach; our job was to learn. The teacher knows his or her job and you had better learn yours, or else. The teacher's word was law for students and parents. And if you don't believe that, you just ask god, the principal.

I remember an event from my junior high school years that illustrates the power of the principal. Someone in school had done an "awful," whatever that meant; I sure don't remember now. Anyhow, because no one would take responsibility for his awful act, every boy in school was required to bend over while god, the principal, administered a sharp blow to each boy's bottom with a rather large and heavy paddle. The most harm for the recipients, as I recall, was probably the damage done to their dignity, but the principal's point was well made.

As far as I know or remember, nobody, but no one, ever questioned the principal's authority for such an action. After all you don't mess with a god. You learn respect. Maybe it was a questionable action, I don't know. I survived very well without a problem and learned a little more respect for authority.

Today's parents would go totally crazy. "Not my kid," is the battle cry of today's parents. The six o'clock news station would be called. "My little angel would never do anything wrong" even when the little demons are caught on TV cameras, in classrooms and on school buses, committing their dastardly deeds. "We can't allow public servants to bruise the egos of our most precious little monsters." Attorneys would line up for blocks, drooling over the prospect of a massive class action lawsuit against the school board, the governor, the school janitor, the television news station, the newspaper delivery boy and anyone else that might catch their attention. This virtually gives today's school children the license to run the schools and to carry guns to class to enforce any rules they choose, including scaring the bejeebers out of most of the people who are trying to help them learn such a simple thing as respect. What we have now is like having the crazies running the mental institutions, and

everybody loses. These people have little or no respect for anything -- especially themselves. What a shame!

So much for blowing off a little steam. Let's get back to remembering the good old days. Me querulous? Nah.

Holidays, and special occasions always trigger memories of good times long since gone. My birthday is in February, and at one time we called February the

President's month. I felt so fortunate to be born the same month as Washington and Lincoln, each with his own holiday. Today we have one day called President's Day. Even Martin Luther King, Jr. has a birthday to be celebrated in February. Rarely are any of these birthdays celebrated on their actual birth date, but moved around to give the general populace another three-day weekend.

Easter was a time for a school vacation, Easter egg hunts, dressing up and going to Sunday school on Easter Sunday. Now, schools have a "spring break" which is not to be confused with any religious holiday, -- Heaven forbid. Later on, during my formative years, there were Easter Sunrise Services. Now it's "Good Lord, is the sun up already?"

June was for proms and girls and the beginning of long days of good weather, swimming holes, girls, soft-ball, basketball, and girls. Now it's WifeBud and I speculating about how many too-damned-hot days we will have this year and trying to keep up the fitness program mentioned earlier -- elbow bends, arm raises and wrist turns.

July Fourth, Independence Day, parades, steaks on

the barbecue, picnics, fireworks, baseball, and lots of noise. Now it's a well-done hamburger, hold the onions, turn on the TV, grab the Tums and adjust the hearing aids. "Hon, where did I leave my hearing aids?"

Labor Day, last big weekend of the summer. More barbecues, picnics and baseball. Try to squeeze in everything that has been put off, as in "we'll do that later." Now it's loads of salads, watch those onions, and if we're lucky, maybe a baseball game on TV.

Thanksgiving. Lots of family, lots of get-togethers, lots of memories shared, lots of food. Football -- let the good times roll. Now it's scattered families. My generation seems to be shrinking (it's getting lonely at the top of this pyramid). Some of us senior survivors gather together and reminisce. "Would you prefer the Milk of Magnesia or the Tums?" Crummy football game. Maybe we could move to Puerto Rico where they have year 'round baseball. Naah.

Christmas. The grandest of all the holidays. Family, anticipation, stockings, presents, excitement, food. Now it's grandchildren scattered across the country, each

expecting an expensive gift, but never writing a Thank You note (a what?). "Don't think about it too much or you could become depressed. Have some more food and maybe some of that Pink Stuff. It will help settle your stomach."

New Years. New beginnings. Ring out the old. Ring in the new. Champagne at midnight. Morning after. Auld lang syne means "fondly remembered times." Now it's get to bed at the usual time --early. Can't handle the booze or late hours any more. Whatever happened to Geritol? "Good night, Dear." "Happy New Year, Love."

Reminiscences. Those good old days.

For some of the senior single folks, widowed or divorced, these holidays can be even more awkward. My next door neighbor had a very disappointing Christmas this past year. It seems that he visited some close relatives and their families. The story goes that he and one of his close relatives got into a disagreement over some very minor incident; something like, "You forgot to say 'Excuse me'," that led to the brink of WWIII. C'mon folks, it's Christmas. Peace!

One of my wife's dearest friends, and my JanBud, has been a widow for about thirty years. She is one remarkable lady. Her closest relative lives about 2,000 miles away in the middle of ice and snow and wind and cold. JanBud stays near home at Christmas time and always remains cheerful and upbeat while she visits other people in similar circumstances, spreading joy and love as she goes. She's some kind of lady!

Life and remembrances are what you make them. . .
you try not to dwell on regrets regarding this lifetime but
you're already making plans for your next lifetime.

✓ (Learn to play a musical instrument; write more, <u>talk</u>
<u>less</u>; <u>refrain from giving advice unless someone really</u>
<u>begs for it</u>; take better care of the body).

You know you're getting older when . . .

. . . you can remember attending live programs with Spike Jones, Red Skelton, Harry James, and many others.

. . . you remember that movies were meant to be entertaining *and relaxing.*

. . . you remember you had a crush on Shirley Temple. Later Elizabeth Taylor completely stole your heart.

. . . you watch girls' skirts blowing in the wind and the only thing you can think of is an old Marilyn Monroe movie.

. . . you realize it's hard to be nostalgic when you forgot to press the "Memory Save" button.

ELEVEN

The Twentieth Century, the age of . . .

When I came into this world, most of the first third of the twentieth century was recent history. I arrived just as the "Great Depression" was getting into full swing. From what I understand, life was pretty simple then, but what did I know, I was just a little kid, having been born at a very early age.

From today's perspective, the history of this century can be quite fascinating. The century started with trains and horses as the major modes of transportation. Horses had been around since about Day One, but the train was a relatively new contraption, having been invented in the previous couple of hundred years, give or take a decade or two. Then along came the automobile, which a lot of people thought was just another passing fancy -- like electric lights and telephones. And like those items, it seemed to catch on, even long before the invention of highways.

Then in the second decade of this century, most of the civilized (?) world was involved in a major world war. Wars are great ways to promote inventions of progress -- new and uncivilized ways to kill one another.

After the "War to end all wars", it was "party time," except someone outlawed booze, and what's a party without booze. Prohibition, speakeasies, flappers, bath-tub gin, ladies in funny looking hats, crime and crime busters, Model T Fords, and finally, the Wall Street Crash. Since hindsight is generally pretty accurate, I would venture that this decade of the Roaring Twenties was kind of a precursor of events and attitudes that would get into full swing later in the century. In that regard, consider this for my later reference: The Model T Ford was the most prolific vehicle around. It was wonderful transportation that could move faster than most horses, even at 27 mph, and could carry a considerably heavier load, without the benefit of reasonable roads or gasoline stations on every street corner.

The Thirties were generally hard times around the

country, and much of the world was in a major financial depression. My family was one of the more fortunate ones; not that we had money, but we had a large farm for growing livestock and crops, and no mortgage. Even then, I remember my dad taking what rare work he could get for a dollar a day, to pay for clothes, taxes, store goods, and other items only acquired with cash. We even had an old car (mentioned in "Those Good Old Days"). The old car was definitely not a speedster, not at 35 mph, but it generally got us there and back, especially with a few select words of encouragement from Dad, spoken under his breath because of Mom's delicate hearing ability. "Watch your language; there is a lady and children present," she would say very sternly. (Snickering heard in the back seat).

World War II took up the first half of the Forties. We, the people, learned how to go faster and farther, and how to kill more of our fellow people with greater efficiency. Speed was gaining more and more of our attention. "Hurry up and win the war so what's left of our troops can rush home again." The second half of the Forties brought the troops home again and they all flopped into bed with the female of the species and that's why we have Baby Boomers this very day. The late Forties were a period of other kinds of building too. A gazillion houses were built for all those Baby Boomers and the populace built roads and cars and everyone was on the move, rushing hither, thither and yon.

The Fifties brought us Korea, the Forgotten War. It wasn't declared to be a war, but don't tell that to the people who got maimed or seriously dead in the "police action." This was also the beginning of the jet airplane era where people learned how to kill other people faster than ever before. The fifties also brought us rock'n roll (whoopee), fast food, faster cars with tail fins and the beginnings of massive freeway systems. Everybody got into a major rush just to get stuck in freeway traffic.

With the Sixties came flower power, free love and bigger and faster modes of transportation. The space race (with that speed word again) was on. Before the end of the decade, the United States landed a man on the moon and returned him safely to earth just like President John

F. Kennedy requested. Can you truly imagine how fast 17,000 miles per hour is? It's difficult for me. My very own first car was a 1942 Pontiac coupe, that I somehow managed to buy in 1952. It could zip right along at about seventy miles per hour -- downhill -- with a tail wind; what a thrill that was. With that old Pontiac as a reference, how can you relate that to 17,000 mph? Anyhow, commercial airline jet travel was also getting a good start in that era. Speed - gotta get there in a hurry. Then there was Viet Nam. Better and faster ways of killing people.

Everyone traveled in the seventies. Jet airfares were cheap. The world was calling. You could get there in a hurry and be back before anybody noticed that you were gone. If you hadn't been to Europe or Hawaii or some other exotic location in the seventies, you could almost count on someone at the office taking up a collection for you to go -- you poor, deprived stay-at-home thing, you. Then the "gasoline crunch" of 1974 hit and the price per gallon jumped astronomically and then, all of a sudden, there is more gas available than ever, and we are off and running again. Got to get there! And make it quick! Damn the torpedoes (or gas prices) full speed ahead! Move it! Hurry! Hurry!

Personal computers made their big debut in the Eighties. Got to catch up. We haven't got time to be messing around waiting on anything and certainly not for some machine to crunch a bunch of numbers. We need bigger, faster, better, now! More bells and more whistles! Gotta have the latest technology! Buttons, switches, indicator lights, black boxes. (At one time, I thought that the push-button radio was one of the greatest inventions to ever come down the pike.)

"Hey we need more of those high-tech black boxes down here! Don't forget to carry your beeper; we might need you in a hurry."

Beepers aren't fast enough; gotta have a cell phone; this is the Nineties. Just think of all those incredibly important phone calls you can make while your latest model, bigger and better, Sport Utility Vehicle is cruising down the road at ninety miles an hour, about to get stuck in freeway traffic "How dare that dummy wreck his car up ahead when I'm in this terrible hurry! Let's move it people! I have more important things to do than anybody; I mean ANY BODY." Road Rage. Uh oh, ambulances. "Hey, up there, do your dying on your own £@#%& time. I'm in a hurry." More road rage.

"Just gotta take a vacation and get some relief from all this stress." Hurry to an overcrowded vacation spot, push the limits, live on the edge, get the adrenaline pumping. Skydiving, hang-gliding, white-water rafting, bungee jumping. Toys! More toys! Jet skis, snowmobiles, all-terrain vehicles, speedboats -- anything as long as it has massive power and speed. Stay until the last possible moment, don't want to miss anything. Big push to get home on time, more road rage, gotta get back to making the big bucks And the cycle goes on. Not much changes, except the names and locations.

Even so-called "relaxation" has become a bit crazy. Now you can buy a television set larger than some old theater screens. They have 900 channel capabilities multiple VCR's and an armful of remote controls so a person can surf dozens of channels at any one given time

-- and never understand what is occurring on any of them. (I exaggerate just a little).

Stephen R. Covey, the author of "The Seven Habits of Highly Effective People," wrote an article for USA Weekend, a Sunday newspaper supplement, in which he proposed how a person could "regain quality time." He writes **"Americans -- the most time-deprived people in the world -- have convinced themselves that despite all the high-tech time-saving devices at their disposal, they are doomed to terminal busy-ness"**[sic] [see note 1]. By my interpretation of this article, there is some new astro-physical quirk in the celestial clock and only a portion of the North American continent experiences a serious time warp like nowhere else in the world. Einstein's theories regarding time have been shot full of holes.

Dr. Covey suggests we should "Pay someone to do your laundry and your yard work for a savings of 14 minutes; be prepared for meetings, nine minutes saved" (and I thought that was just good, common sense and courtesy; silly, old fashioned me); "pay bills electronically, three and one-half minutes saved; use a cell phone, three minutes saved;" (and my favorite) "get up earlier, five minutes saved." The list goes on until a total of sixty minutes are "saved" so you can then "spend" them doing what you really want to do.

I have a counter-proposal. While driving, allow someone to cut in front of you, time used ten seconds max; smile and say a kind hello to a total stranger, time used about six seconds; (and one of my favorites) when you are in a crowded elevator say so all can hear, "The reason I called this meeting today is to wish you a _____(Merry Christmas, Happy Valentine Day, Happy Groundhog Day, a Pleasant Journey, a Nice Day, etc., etc.), time used insignificant because you couldn't make the elevator go any faster regardless; do a kind deed for a friend without letting them know who did it, time used a few seconds to a few minutes; call a shut-in, time used five minutes; and with the remainder of Dr. Covey's sixty minutes saved, take a child for a walk and buy an ice cream; or just "Practice Random Kindness and Senseless Acts of Beauty." You will feel a whole lot better for any of these than you ever will in trying to "squeeze another minute out of your jam-packed day." Everyone has the same amount of available time, it's your attitude towards its use that is so important. Life is for living and enjoying, not racing through.

This century, especially the second half, has been filled with phenomenal advances in most areas of life. Economic standards of living, health and general well-being, technology, communications, spirituality, and a dozen other aspects of existence have improved for the vast majority of the populace. But at what price? Childhood is no longer for children; now it's how fast can we get them "up to speed."

One of the places where this is most apparent is with toy retailers. They sell very few toys for little children but promote high-tech toys that appeal to adult manufacturers and advertisers, who in turn sell to adult parents, albeit through advertising to children. If it's on the television, we have just got to have it. And television is not for children, although most parents plop their kids in front of the tube to watch adult programs so they won't have to be inconvenienced by taking care of those children.

Today's young people think they *have to* be up to date on the latest technology and most early teens know more about computers (and especially computer games) than I will ever learn even if I live to be 150 years old. But then I didn't have a "fast-track" to climb onto when I was their age.

This is the Age of Acceleration and I don't know where it will lead us or if and how it will end. It seems to me that it's like a runaway train or a car that is on the verge of being out of control going down a steep hill. For a while it's a thrill; for a while it's an adrenaline high, "Faster, faster, we want to go faster." But what happens if and when control is lost? Will we find a runaway truck lane where we can safely pull over and regroup? Or will this wild ride end in disaster like so many out-of-control adventures? How many must "lose the ride" in the name of adventure? We have a wonderful world and life is so precious; it's not to be wasted, for any reason.

If you really want to see this wonderful world we live in, take a walk with a two year old -- but don't wait too long because that two year old already has one foot about to step on to the fast track, thanks mostly to parents who don't take the time to slow down and enjoy the sights and wonders a two year old will discover for them. Yes, I believe this is the Age of Acceleration -- too bad too, because there are such marvelous things to discover while spending a little time with a small child: woolly worms, spider webs, dirt and a water hose to make mud, a stray dog, bird poop, bottle tops, rocks and sticks, and incredible amounts of other really neat stuff. What a joy it is to experience discovering the world through the eyes of a child. Excuse me, while I go find one of my younger grandchildren.

You know you're getting older when . . . .

. . . you can remember when common sense was instilled, taught and encouraged, and didn't need to be legislated.

Note 1: Excerpts from "Chop An Hour from Your Day" by Stephen R. Covey, from the January 22-24, 1999 issue of USA Weekend was used with permission from Franklin Covey Co. All rights reserved..

«««««   »»»»»»

As an adjunct, consider these tidbits of information:
The Wright Brothers' first airplane flight in 1903 lasted 12
seconds, for 120 feet, at a mind-boggling 7 miles per hour.
Cross country aircraft travel in 1935 took 5 or 6 days and nights
to go between New York and Los Angeles.

In 1945 it took 18 to 20 hours. In 1955 it took 8 to 9 hours.
In 1965 it took 5 to 6 hours.   Still does.
Since then, the only meaningful measure lies in the time to and
from the airport, waiting in various lines, recovering from time
zone changes, and handling luggage.

The U S Department of Defense now wants to build the
"HyperSoar" which will fly at 7,000 mph at an altitude of
130,000 feet and go between New York and Tokyo in two hours.
You don't even want to think about jet-lag or luggage.

(Thanks to Larry Dwyer, Scott Willey & John Lake at Aviation
History On-Line Museum for the tidbits. Check their web site at
www.aviation-history.com)

«««««   »»»»»»

100

TWELVE

Goin' back

When I was about six years old, and just starting school, my parents decided they would see how many different places they could live in one lifetime. I went to first grade in three separate schools and a total of thirteen schools before finally graduating from high school. This entire process involved back and forth moves between just three counties -- in three scattered states.

Then, I began college but dropped out before "dropping out" was the fashionable thing to do. I convinced myself I was doing my patriotic duty by serving my country in the United States Navy. Mostly, I was tired of school and just wanted a change of scenery. Then, one of the first things the Navy did was send me to school. What else.

During my tour of Naval duty, I was moved from

one station to a ship, then to another ship and then to a third ship. Meanwhile, those ships were not exactly stationary and I got to see the top of a lot of ocean. I made two tours of the Orient to such exotic places as Japan, Korea, Hong Kong, the Philippines and numerous other hunks of dirt between these locations. I love to travel -- still do.

After the Navy and I parted ways, I still could not settle down in one place for an extended period of time. There remained a restlessness that I couldn't seem to shake. WifeOne was a real stay-at-home, so we were doomed from the start (for a wide variety of other reasons, too) and that marriage ended in divorce.

Much later, I met, courted for four years, and finally married my WifeSoulMateBuddy. She likes to see what is around the next corner or over the next hill, just as I do. We have traveled quite a bit, including Europe, Scandinavia, North Africa, New Zealand, Australia, Mexico, Alaska, and several trips to most of the Hawaiian Islands. The whole point of this section is not to turn into a travelogue, but to mention one minor trip.

WifeBud and I decided to visit one of her girl friends from years gone by. We would make a grand tour and visit some of our offspring scattered around the country. As luck would have it, WifeBud's girl friend lived within 75 miles of where I grew up -- where it all started and where I still had a couple of long lost relatives that I hadn't seen or heard from in about forty years. What a neat thing it would be for me to drive back to the old "homestead" while the ladies caught up on chatting about old times (this is no place for a husband).

So I borrowed a car and set off to revisit the days of my youth. I arrived in the village, parked in front of the only church and began a stroll down memory lane. That church was where I learned a lot of pretty neat things, good old-fashioned Sunday School stuff that established a foundation for the values that I still try to live by today. The next thing I noticed was that a large number of the houses were deserted and falling down, but I could still remember the names of the people who had lived in many of them all those decades ago. I walked a mile or so and came to the house where my great-

Ancestors

grand-mother had lived with my great-aunt and uncle. I remembered playing in great-grandma's wheelchair on the porch and watching my great-aunt operate the old telephone company -- the kind with the crank handles to make the party-line phones ring.

Then I walked by the house where I was born and spent the first years of my life. What a depressing looking place it was after all those years. It only vaguely resembled the place in my memory. Nearby was the house where one of my favorite great-aunts had lived alone. I almost didn't recognize it, because it had fallen down and was overgrown with vegetation. The one store in the village had been torn down many years earlier. The railroad tracks that had gone through the village, next to the creek, had been torn out and removed. I didn't know that abandoned tracks were ever removed; what an insult to nostalgia.

I walked by the three-room school building where I had started my educational journey. They still had swings out back. Unfortunately, I could not remember the names of any of the teachers, but I knew the name of the prettiest girl in my class -- Bonnie (it figures I would remember). Now, I could look in the windows and see signs of growing and learning and little ones.

Finally, I went to the cemetery where my father, his father, my grand-mother, my great-grand-mother and most of her daughters were buried. I read a lot the head-stones. Some of the names I recognized, most I didn't. There was no one there. I said goodbye to no one in particular and I left, closing the gate behind me.

Depressing journey.

Some times you just can't go back.

THIRTEEN

Secrets of a happy partnership

WifeSoulMateBud and I have been in a formal marriage partnership for almost thirty years now. We got married then we lived together -- how terribly old-fashioned (you're showing your age again). We each had a previous marriage, each of which lasted about 15 years, plus we each endured several years of single status. After an extended courtship, we finally married. Many of our relatives and friends believe that we now have just about a perfect relationship -- and I would tend to agree with that. She tells me where to go and what to do, and I go and I do it (just kidding, honey).

One of the major reasons for our marital bliss is that each of us take our marriage vows very seriously. To take each other, to have and to hold, in sickness and in health, for richer or for poorer (I'm tired of being poorer, let's switch to a healthy level of rich), forsaking all others; and all that other good stuff. We have discussed our "intolerables" and we trust that the other will not violate those intolerables. Mostly, we like as well as love each other. We also have some clearly-defined job descriptions: He takes out the trash and climbs on the roof as needed; she cooks dinner and keeps the fridge well stocked with good stuff. He does a fair share of household chores.

Like a lot of couples that have been married for any considerable time, we also have developed our own private language. Earlier, I mentioned "yucky" as being a familiar expression. WifeBud also likes such expressions as "baby" airplane, (meaning any small single engine aircraft -- as opposed to a jet airliner) or "baby" computer or "baby" air conditioner, or "baby" anything small. (That baby airplane never did grow up to be a 747, for shame). Also, so much of our conversation consists of half sentences, "Did you go to the . . ." "Yes, and I got the . . ." "Good, we'll save it for . . ." "Why not . . ?" "Okay, but . . ." "Oh, . . ." And it all makes perfect sense -- at least to us. Then there are those times when one person will be thinking about a certain topic and the other person will verbalize it without any outward clues. Spooky. I can't get away with a thing.

Private language is particularly helpful when you are in public, or in the company of other people. When WifeBud was going through "the ladies' change" (a.k.a. menopause) I used to hear a lot of "Don't you think it's unseasonably warm at the moment?" This translates as "I'm so hot I could die." Then there is "I feel a real 'swassle' coming on," meaning the grand-daddy of all burps is in dire need of being expressed. There are lots of other little endearing, and sometimes humorous, expressions that identify us as a couple.

We have always been supportive of each others' views, opinions, values, dreams, ambitions and space. We have also valued our time of togetherness, one-ness, similarities, and differences (viva la difference). Never once has either of us used a phrase I have heard used in many other relationships such as, "It's all your fault, you stupid dummy." Not that there haven't been occasions where it could have seemed appropriate, but because that's neither loving nor supportive. We seem to agree, at some unspoken level, that it's best to look for love, not faults.

I remember very well one of our most wonderful trips when we could have had a "your fault" episode. We were just finishing up a perfect six week vacation "Down Under." We had gone "independent" in Australia and had taken an organized tour in New Zealand. On the last day of the tour, the itinerary for the following day read "depart Auckland." We arrived at the airport early, reluctant but ready for the long trip back to the States. The counter for our airlines was small and deserted, so I checked with the terminal office. They couldn't understand my problem until they checked my ticket and informed me we were early all right -- a full day early. When I informed WifeBud of our "dilemma," we stood in the middle of the terminal building and howled with laughter. Instead of being upset, we laughed, and I'm sure we looked pretty ridiculous to the other travelers. Then, we thoroughly enjoyed another full day in Auckland. As an added bonus, we also received a night of free lodging because we had used one chain of hotels enough nights to qualify for a freebie.

We were married for quite a few years before the word "retirement" ever entered our vocabulary. WifeBud "retired" first, meaning she gave up a regular income and took early retirement, so we could start a new business in a far-removed, new for us, location. You might say that wasn't a true retirement, that was the beginning of a lot of work. We learned we could work very well together, something a lot of couples have not learned how to manage.

So often, women will complain about men hanging around the house all the time with nothing to do. Retirees, men and women, need to learn early that a spouse is not responsible for their partner's entertainment and well-being. We're back to that business of finding an avocation. Be responsible for yourself. I have a BoatBud, a FishBud, a BaseballBud and a ComputerBud. WifeBud has her bridge ladies and library. We can choose to spend time together or time with outside interests. Both are good.

Some seniors spend far too much time worrying about things they cannot control, e.g., income, outgo, whether Social Security will still be viable long after they are gone, where will they go if California falls into the ocean, who will save Medicare and why must HMO rates keep going up. I think it would be a much wiser expenditure of energy to give attention to things you can change. For

example: How do you want to be remembered?

I went to a seminar a number of years ago where the instructor asked that question and then asked each of us to write down up to five words that we would want on our tombstone. I knew my five words immediately, without giving it any thought (Sorry, but that's personal for a while longer). I have collected a few of the more fun and interesting ideas over the years and here is a sampling:

> The gun was not loaded.
>
> It was safe sex.
>
> Please call before you dig. (WifeBud)
>
> Her husband never suspected.
>
> Health Care is for Sissies
>
> See - It wasn't psychosomatic
>
> (Candace Pert - see Note 1 below)
>
> Rest In Peace Adrenaline Junkie.
>
> I had the right-of-way.
>
> It wasn't worth worrying about.

It's a fun exercise which can give you a clue to your values and/or sense of humor. Give it a try -- and lighten up a little.

_____   _____   _____   _____   _____

Now consider this for a moment: If you're alive, your reason for being on this earth has not been completed. If you're not, carefully put this book down and reverently move toward the light.

Note 1: Candace Pert is the author of *Molecules of Emotion* (Scribner. New York 1997)

FOURTEEN

Looking back, looking forward

Those of us who consider ourselves to be "Pre-Baby Boomers," those of us born in the Twenties, Thirties and early Forties, have witnessed a lot of change along the way. We were born and reared before the advent of television, plastic, a space program, fast food, credit cards, electronic wizardry of incredible variety, split atoms, word processors, flying saucers, skate boards, instant coffee, Social Security payments, and millions of wonders of the new religion called Technology.

We were born in a time of trust, when you could leave the house without locking all the doors and windows. We knew our neighbors and were there to help them when they were in need and they did the same for us. People were honest and trustworthy; a handshake had meaning. Young people were taught to be courteous, obedient and respectful of people and property. Most of us went to church on Sunday. We recited the Pledge of Allegiance every day in school and at most other meetings, and we knew it had meaning. We respected the laws of the land

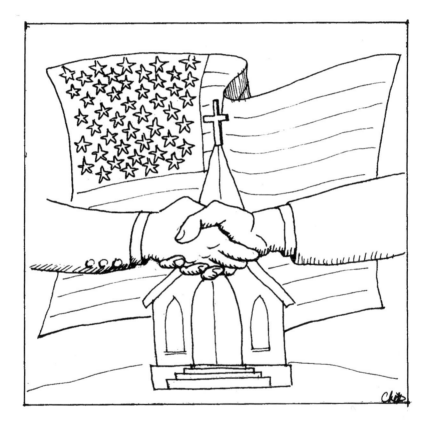

and avoided trouble at all costs. We knew and appreciated the value of money. We weren't perfect by any means, but most of us aspired to be.

All of that is going to sound hopelessly old fashioned, or an equivalent term in modern jargon, to those folks who came into this world after World War II. That's okay; just please consider some of these ideas. Attitudes began to change dramatically in the late 50's and early 60's, just about the time television was becoming a common household item, hmmm.

Trust was lost, watch out for yourself, every one is out to get you. Avoid your neighbors and don't get involved in any of their problems, even if you could save a life or prevent a crime. Courtesy is for you old people; up yours. Obey the law of the jungle, get them before they get you. Respect is no longer something to consider, self or otherwise -- Show respect, why should I, they don't respect me. Reverence -- to hell with it, let's go burn a flag. The laws are for people dumb enough to get caught; anybody can get a gun. So what if we have a bunch of maxed-out credit cards -- we'll just get more cards or file bankruptcy -- no big deal.

Somewhere along the way, we started giving up our

responsibilities. Unfortunately, because you can't have one without the other, we were also giving up freedoms when we reneged on responsibilities in favor of "Let the government take care of my problems." As an example, let's go back to the automobile analogy: We, the current auto buying public, want bigger and faster cars but we do not want to drive any more responsibly. We want to go faster, drive recklessly, endangering our lives and the lives of those around us, and even do some driving while drinking. But we don't want to take responsibility for our actions. We petition the government to enforce laws about having safer cars -- more auto safety equipment, seat belts, air bags, etc., etc. The underlying message of this public outcry is, "Government, save me from my stupidity and irresponsibility." The government, being responsive to the people, requires more safety measures to be added to the vehicles, at considerable additional costs to the consumers, who then feel secure for the moment, and drive like bigger idiots, and then the cycle starts all over again.

By avoiding our responsibilities, we the public, feel

we have to sue whoever we feel should be held responsible, whether it be a neighbor, manufacturer, installer, organization, school, doctor or just someone who got into the line of sight. As a result, there are more attorneys per capita in the United States, by far, than any other country in the world. This raises the costs of just about everything and makes a grand mess of the courts.

About this time, the "greed monster" rears its ugly head, and everyone wants to have as much, or more, than his neighbor. Never mind how this is going to be accomplished, we want all of the latest goodies and toys. If a kid's hero has $200 tennis shoes, he thinks he should have them also, even if he has to bonk somebody over the head to get them. If I can put this deal together by pretending to be a religious zealot, more power to me. If this corporation can slide by with faulty merchandise or toxic chemicals to get a bigger and better bottom line, more power to us, and that's why we have this huge, incredible staff of attorneys. We just make the guns, the tobacco and booze, the television programs, the X-rated material; we don't tell kids to buy it.

At one time, we the people, were totally responsible for our safety, income, security, homes, children and all other aspects of our lives. Parents took the role of parenting very seriously and they felt responsible if their child were to cross the line. I feel that until we return to some semblance of this responsibility, our beautiful country and our world, are destined to continue on a downhill trend, as predicted by some folks. Some of the soothsayers, current or ancient, have been predicting massive and disastrous calamities for the turn of the millennium. I believe if such events were to occur, it would be because we brought it all upon ourselves with our attitudes.

We have survived the Sixties, the Seventies, the Eighties and the Nineties. We are headed for a new century and the "Oughts," as in "ought one -- 01." (In Britain, that would be the "Naughts" and we could call them the "Naughties." WifeBud had me say that. See what I put up with?).

(All right now, serious up for a big finish)

Those of us who are currently Senior Citizens have seen and experienced a great deal. And we survived. I believe this old world will keep on chugging along, with or without the soothsayers. I also believe that a very large contingent of Senior Citizens of my era will be right here to witness all these events, because

we are survivors!!

So give thanks for the tenacity of life
and the joys of living.
And say a little prayer for the next
generation of senior citizens.

There is no standing still.

You're going forward or slipping back.

When we quit running, we start rusting.

When we quit growing, we start rotting.

Life never stands still. Life is to be lived.

James Dillet Freeman *

You know you're getting older when . . . **you realize just how strong the survival instinct is.**

* James Dillet Freeman quoted with permission.

'Tovers . . . . . .

In an endeavor such as this, a writer gets to the end and realizes he has some material left over that he really wanted to use but there just wasn't space. So in this case, we'll add a page or two and call it "Tovers" -- short for leftovers.

'TOVERS

While many of us have Senior Moments, my lovely step-daughter says she has "Junior Moments." Same idea.

You know you're getting older when . . .

. . . you look forward to another dull, quiet evening at home.

. . . getting lucky means you can remember where you parked your car.

. . . you can remember when you could buy clothing that was NOT a mobile advertising media and Nike was just the ancient goddess of victory.

. . . [one last golden oldie] you wander into a room and wonder why you entered it, then you leave that room and wonder why you left. That's a Senior Moment.

. . . you are no longer a slave to fashion. "If you don't like mixed plaids plus stripes and dots, and mismatched socks, you can just look elsewhere."

"Oh yeah, well your mother dresses you funny too."

We would like to hear from you!

Send us your comments regarding this book and your "Senior Moments" stories. Please include your name, address, phone, e-mail address and permission to re-print your stories and comments. Send to:

Don Core - SOFITS Publishing
P.O. Box 65235
Vancouver, WA 98665
Phone: (360) 694-5785
Fax: (360) 693-4653
e-mail: coredk@spiritone.com
www.coredk-books.com

Thank you!

314 EMPLOYMENT WANTED

314 EMPLOYMENT WANTED

CREATIVE GENIUS has completed a masterpiece worthy of literary acclaim and months on someone's best-seller list. Seeking high income, low energy, part-time executive position. Background includes a hundred years as an entrepreneur, businessman, seminar writer-instructor, freelance-writer, co-publisher, and former "baby airplane" pilot.

I can make the tough executive decisions, earn the $2Mil bonus and still have time for my afternoon nap. Call today, talent like this MUST be expressed and rewarded. Call between 10 A.M. and 11 A.M. or between 3 P.M. and 3:30 P.M. (If an old grump answers, hang up). Call (360)694-5785 or send offers to Don Core, PO Box 65235, Vancouver WA 98665

Limited time offer. (I'm not getting any younger).

ARTISTIC MASTERMIND has to create funny cartoons and humorous illustrations. This need to feed a creative passion must have an outlet to express major works of humorous art.

Portfolio includes drawings and cartoons on napkins and table tops all over the world, as well as all those items published in trade magazines and newspapers.

Background includes a degree in Journalism and years of experience as a technical writer and illustrator.

I can be reached at the same address/phone as the author of this book. Just let the phone ring loud and long as he tends to doze off. (I'm a late Baby-Boomer with a lot of good years left for creative endeavors).

ORDER FORM

SENIOR MOMENTS makes great gifts any time of year. Order the perfect gift book for friends, relatives, associates.

_____ Copies of "Senior Moments" at $10.95 ea. $_____

Washington State residents add 7.6% Sales Tax $_____

Books shipped USPS Standard Book Rate. Allow ample time for delivery. For Priority Mail delivery, add $3.00.

Sorry, we do not offer credit card sales. You can use your credit cards at your favorite retail book store; have them order this book for you: ISBN # 1-879752-03-4

Send your check or money order, along with your order and complete shipping address, city, state, zip code and phone number (for verification purposes) to:

Don Core - SOFITS Publishing

P.O. Box 65235   Vancouver, WA 98665

Phone: 360-694-5785   Fax: 360-693-4653

e-mail: coredk@spiritone.com

"Satisfaction guaranteed"